THIS IS A GUN

A SAFETY GUIDE
FOR FAMILIES WITH CHILDREN

WRITTEN BY:
DAVID COX (D)

ILLUSTRATED BY:
JOE RUIZ (R)

Copyright © 2026 by David Cox

All rights reserved. No part of this publication may be reproduced, distributed, or transmitted in any form or by any means, including photocopying, recording, or other electronic or mechanical methods, without the prior written permission of the publisher, except in the case of brief quotations embodied in critical reviews and certain other noncommercial uses permitted by copyright law.

Common Ground Press, Charlotte, NC

permissions info@thisisagun.org

For details, contact sales@thisisagun.org

Print ISBN: 979-8-218-76301-5

LCCN: 2025922563

Printed in the United States of America on SFI Certified paper.

First Edition

For more gun safety resources please visit:

www.thisisagun.org

To my children, Hayes and Emerson.
With every lesson I teach, I hope you see that love protects, and learning empowers. This book is one way I love you.

A Letter to Grown-Ups

Dear Parents, Teachers, and Caregivers,

This book was written with one purpose: to keep children safe.

Guns are a reality in many communities. Even if a child never plans to touch a gun, they may still come across one. Knowing what to do in that moment can save a life.

Children deserve honest guidance delivered in a way that is simple, calm, and free of fear.

This book is designed to open conversations, not to replace them. Please take time to talk with your child as you read. Encourage questions. Listen with patience. Reassure them that safety is always the goal.

Unless they are in a supervised training program, children and young people should never touch or handle a gun.

For families who involve youth in hunting, sport shooting, or farm work, firearms should only be handled under careful adult supervision and with proper training.

You know your child best. Some may want to read and move on. Others may need more time, more answers, or more comfort. What matters most is that they hear a consistent message:

Guns are not toys.

If a child ever comes across a gun outside of those settings, the safest choice is to stop, step away, and tell a grown-up immediately.

Thank you for reading this book with care. By choosing to share it, you are helping protect not only your child but every child they may one day influence.

With respect & gratitude,

Dave Cox

For more gun safety resources, please vist:
www.thisisagun.org

What do you do if you see a gun?

1. Do not touch the gun.
2. Run away from it.
3. Tell an adult about the gun.

THERE ARE MANY TYPES OF GUNS.

Guns come in different sizes.
Some guns are small.
Some guns are tall.

All guns are dangerous!

Guns are tools but they can be very dangerous just like a hot stove, a knife, medications or things found under the kitchen sink!

Your parents might own guns and keep them in or around your house.

PARENT NOTE: THESE SCENES SHOW UNSAFE GUN STORAGE/STAGING.
RESPONSIBLE ADULTS SHOULD ALWAYS SECURE FIREARMS SO THEY CANNOT BE ACCESSED OR OPERATED BY A CHILD.

Many different people own guns.

Your parent's might own guns. Your friends' parents might own guns. Maybe your older brothers or sisters might own guns too.

GUNS ARE VERY DANGEROUS AND SHOULD NEVER BE PICKED UP UNLESS YOU ARE WITH AN ADULT.

If you find a gun, what should you do?

PARENT NOTE: THIS SCENE SHOWS UNSAFE GUN STORAGE/STAGING.
RESPONSIBLE ADULTS SHOULD ALWAYS SECURE FIREARMS SO THEY CANNOT BE ACCESSED OR OPERATED BY A CHILD.

1. Do not touch the gun.
2. Run away from it.
3. Tell an adult about the gun.

What if your friend wants to SHOW you a gun?

What do you do?

PARENT NOTE: THIS SCENE SHOWS UNSAFE GUN STORAGE/STAGING. RESPONSIBLE ADULTS SHOULD ALWAYS SECURE FIREARMS SO THEY CANNOT BE ACCESSED OR OPERATED BY A CHILD.

Tell your friend "NO, I DO NOT WANT TO SEE IT".

Leave the room right away and find an adult.

What do you do if your friend is holding a gun?

GET AWAY FROM YOUR FRIEND RIGHT AWAY AND TELL AN ADULT!

Remember!

Guns are Dangerous!

1. Do not touch the gun.
2. Run away from it.
3. Tell an adult about the gun.

MY GUN SAFETY PROMISE

★ I PROMISE:

★ I WILL NEVER TOUCH A GUN.

★ IF I SEE A GUN, I WILL STOP WHAT I'M DOING.

★ I WILL RUN AWAY.

★ I WILL TELL A GROWN-UP.

SIGNED:

I AM A SAFETY HERO!

Gun Library
Top 10 Owned Handguns in the United States

This section is designed to help parents and guardians familiarize children with what real firearms look like.

All images are presented at life-size scale for visual recognition.

The goal is simple: the more children understand that real guns are not toys, the greater their chances of making safe, responsible choices if they ever encounter one in real life.

GLOCK 17

S&W M&P SHIELD

SIG SAUER P365

RUGER LCP

Dave Cox~ Author

A firearms enthusiast with over 20 years of experience and training, and is a certified firearms safety instructor. A father of two and passionate advocate for children's safety, Dave wrote This Is A Gun to help families talk openly and responsibly about firearms. He holds a Bachelor of Science degree from Northeastern University and lives in Charlotte, North Carolina, with his wife and children. Through his work, Dave blends a deep respect for gun ownership with a heartfelt commitment to protecting kids through honest conversation.

Joe Ruiz~ Illustrator

Fine artist, illustrator and author with over thirty years' experience making art. He studied art in Santa Barbara & San Francisco. But art education doesn't end once you leave college, it's a lifelong pursuit of learning new techniques, materials & disciplines. He is a husband and father of two grown children and lives in the bucolic countryside of Central GA.

www.ingramcontent.com/pod-product-compliance
Lightning Source LLC
LaVergne TN
LVRC080724070526
838199LV00041B/733